Libraries can be beautiful as well as educational

Libraries

Joy Frisch

A⁺
Smart Apple Media

COPYRIGHT

❖ Published by Smart Apple Media

1980 Lookout Drive, North Mankato, MN 56003

Designed by Rita Marshall

Copyright © 2003 Smart Apple Media. International copyright reserved in

all countries. No part of this book may be reproduced in any form without

written permission from the publisher.

Printed in the United States of America

❖ Photographs by Richard Cummins, Herbert L. Gatewood, Richard Gross,

Galyn C. Hammond, The Image Finders (Michael Evans, Mark E. Gibson),

Tom Myers, Rainbow (Rob Crandall, Mark E. Gibson), Unicorn (Andre Jenny)

❖ Library of Congress Cataloging-in-Publication Data

Frisch, Joy. Libraries / by Joy Frisch. p. cm. − (Structures)

Summary: Provides an introduction to the history and

purpose of libraries. Includes bibliographical references.

❖ ISBN 1-58340-146-6

1. Libraries−Juvenile literature. [1. Libraries.] I. Title. II. Structures

(North Mankato, Minn.)

Z721 .F75 2002   027−dc21   2001049967

❖ First Edition 9 8 7 6 5 4 3 2 1

$\mathcal{L}$ibraries

CONTENTS

A Building of Books

A building filled with books is called a library. The old French word for book is *liber*. This is where the English word "library" comes from. ❖ Libraries are intended to help people find information. In order to do that, libraries are usually divided into sections. Children have their own special area with children's books and small chairs and tables. Teenagers often have a special section, too. There are also areas with large tables where older students and adults read and study.

Many libraries have a spacious central room

❖ Most libraries are open to the public. This means that anyone can use them. If a person is old enough to write his or her name, he or she can get a library card. The card lets a person borrow books from a library. But it is important to bring those books back on time. Libraries charge fines when books are returned late.

Designing Libraries

People began building libraries a long time ago. The first library was probably a 5,000-year-old collection of clay tablets carved in the area of present-day Iraq, Syria, and Turkey. About

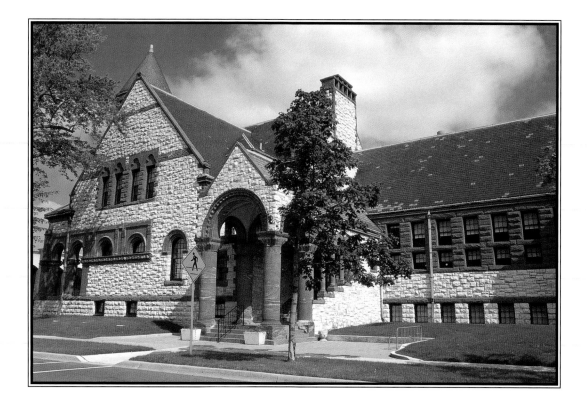

2,300 years ago, the Alexandrian Library in Egypt was one of

the most famous libraries of ancient times. It held more than

400,000 **scrolls**. ❖ Today, almost every town in North

This library is shaped much like a church

Theodor Geisel (Dr. Seuss) Library in San Diego, California

Library
Entrance

America has either a public or school library. A man named

Andrew Carnegie had a lot to do with that. Carnegie was a rich

man who gave money to build some of the first libraries in the

United States. He funded 1,689 public **Many**

Carnegie

libraries. He also built 830 libraries in other **libraries are**

almost 100

English-speaking countries. All of the **years old and**

are still in use

Carnegie libraries have unique **archi- today.**

tecture, so no two look exactly alike. ❖ Many libraries are

famous for their fancy architecture. Some are decorated with

murals, or pictures, painted onto the walls and ceilings. Some

have huge marble columns. Statues, sculptures, and fountains

also decorate many libraries. ❖ Some libraries are small. In

rural towns, the library may be a one-room cottage with a

This library has a simple but elegant design

wood stove. Other libraries have many rooms and thousands of books. The New York Public Library has more books than any other public library in the United States. It cost $9 million to build. More than 10 million people visit and use the library every year.

On the Inside

From the outside, libraries may look different. But inside they are a lot alike. In fact, the most important parts of a library are inside. ❖ Everything and everyone in a library has a purpose. Librarians are the people who work in libraries.

Librarians answer questions and help people locate information.

At the **circulation desk**, they help people check out books to

take home. ❖ Display racks hold newspapers and magazines.

Some libraries loan videos, movies, and musical tapes. **Patrons** use computers to look up information or locate a specific book.

Many libraries have special meeting rooms that are used for story hours or classes. ❖ But it is the bookshelves that take up most of the space in a library. Librarians organize the books on the shelves using the Dewey Decimal System. This numbering system was developed in 1873. Today, it is used in more than 135 countries.

When completed in 1910, the New York Public Library had more than 75 miles (120 km) of bookshelves.

Librarians at work in the Library of Congress

Famous Libraries

Some libraries are quite famous. Presidential libraries are not traditional libraries. Instead of books, they house important papers of U.S. presidents. Since 1939, 10 presidential libraries have been built. ❖ The Ambrosian Library in Milan, Italy, has papers written by scientists and monks. The Bibliotheque Nationale in Paris, France, is one of the world's largest libraries. It began in the 1300s as the royal library of King Charles V. The ancient

Some libraries in the United States fly three flags outside: one each for the national, state, and local government.

Alexandrian Library no longer exists, but Egypt is now

building a new library where the old one once stood. ❖ The

Library of Congress in Washington, D.C., is the national library

The Library of Congress looks like a temple

of the United States. It was built in 1800. Because it has a **copyright** role, it receives one copy of every book that is copyrighted in the United States. It houses more than 14 million books! ❖ Whether fancy or simple, large or small, a library is a good place to read and think. No matter what they look like, all libraries

About 100 years ago, many of America's first public libraries were in city halls and police and fire departments.

help us to learn and discover more about the world around us.

Libraries may have statues of important people

Exploring Libraries

A trip to your local library will help you become familiar with the services your library offers. There is much to learn and discover at libraries.

What You Need

A notebook

A pencil

A library card

What You Do

Go to your local library (ask an adult to go with you). Walk around and find the different sections of the library. Find the children's section. Find the circulation desk where you can check out books. Does the library have computers to use? If you do not have a library card, have an adult help you get one from a librarian. Check out some books that interest you. Make a list of the different sections of the library. Besides books, find out what other items you can borrow.

Even small libraries are fun places to explore

Index

Words to Know

architecture (AR-ki-tek-chur)—the character, style, and structure of a building

circulation desk (sur-kyoo-LAY-shun desk)—the desk where books are checked out
and returned

copyright (KAH-pee-rite)—protection offered to authors of books so that no one
copies or steals their writing

Dewey Decimal System (DOO-wee DEH-seh-mul sis-tum)—a system of numbers
used by libraries to classify and organize books

patrons (PAY-truns)—the people who use a service or program

scrolls (SKROLLS)—rolls of paper with writing on them

Read More

Fowler, Allan. *The Dewey Decimal System.* New York: Children's Press, 1996.

Jones, Theodore. *Carnegie Libraries Across America.* New York: John Wiley & Sons,
1997.

Raatma, Lucia. *Libraries.* New York: Children's Press, 1998.

Internet Sites

History of Andrew Carnegie and
Carnegie Libraries
http://www.andrewcarnegie.cc

New York Public Library:
On-Lion for Kids
http://www2.nypl.org/home/branch/kids